How to Cook Healthy in a Hurry: 50 Quick and Easy, Low Fat Recipes You Can Make In 30 Minutes

Helen Cassidy Page

What Reviewers Are Saying

5.0 out of 5 stars
In a world of hurry this works!
This book "How to Cook Healthy in a Hurry"
will make my top 5 list of meal time go to
helpers. Love the Fig and Raspberry parfait!
And fast to prepare too! You just gotta have this
on ready at hand for meal time.
Levi Foote

5.0 out of 5 stars
Jam packed with recipes!!
Who knew eating healthy could taste so good! I
love dips and there were a couple that looked
very simple to make. Can't wait to try more!
Patricia T.

5.0 out of 5 stars
Quick and Easy!
As a single dad with four hungry kids, I am
always looking for ways to "Cook Healthy in a
Hurry"! So the title caught my attention
immediately. I can see from the instructions that
they are very quick and easy to make
(sometimes even more important than being
delicious). I am excited to try these out on my
kids because they are getting tired of my same
old limited menu.

In the time it takes me to cook a hamburger helper, I could have a much healthier meal for my family.
Matson

Give How To Cook Healthy A Thumbs Up

Most cooks agree that a cookbook is worth the price if you find even one recipe that becomes a favorite. I hope you will find many recipes that will please you and make your kitchen life easier. If you do, please help me spread the word about How to Cook Healthy in a Hurry. Tell your friends and please give it a positive review Amazon by going to this link:

http://www.amazon.com/kindle-store/dp/B00AP980WG

Happy Eating

Helen

Free Gift For You

Before we get started, check out the How To Cook Healthy website below to get my gift to you of 5 free, delicious, sugar free dessert recipes and receive updates, promotions and tidbits you will enjoy.

http://www.helencassidypage.com/how-to-cook-healthy-in-a-hurry-bonus/

Get all the How To Cook Healthy In A Hurry books

How To Cook Healthy In A Hurry, Volume 2

http://www.amazon.com/How-Cook-Healthy-Hurry-ebook/dp/B00C3OHEGE/

The Healthy Husband Cookbook

http://www.amazon.com/The-Healthy-Husband-Cookbook-ebook/dp/B00BEBOW8K/

The Soup Diet Cookbook

HOW TO COOK HEALTHY IN A HURRY

http://www.amazon.com/Soup-Diet-Cookbook-Delicious-ebook/dp/B00BRRZQC2/

Table of Contents

My name is Helen Cassidy Page and for almost 40 years I have been teaching cooking and writing about food. In all those years, there is one thing I hear over and over. *Helen, I want to feed my family great meals, but I don't have time!*

LET MY 40 YEARS OF EXPERIENCE SOLVE THAT PROBLEM

Whether you are a kitchen ninja or a wanna-be-chef trying to figure out the difference between a spatula and a cell phone, you need fast and delicious recipes that will make mealtime easier, healthier and happier. Am I right?

How to Cook Healthy in a Hurry is not just a cookbook. It is a cooking course, where, in 50 delicious recipes for soups, salads, main courses and desserts, you will learn my secrets and tips to help you transform dinnertime from a chore to a pleasure.

HOW TO COOK HEALTHY IN A HURRY WILL TEACH YOU . . .

- To choose and read recipes for mealtime success
- To adjust recipes to suit your own tastes
- To make smart shortcuts when shopping and cooking
- To read labels to avoid ingredients that can harm you
- To choose kitchen helpers that are good for you
- To use the 80-20 Rule
- To stock your pantry, outfit your Healthy in a Hurry kitchen and use the best cooking methods to make prep, cooking and cleanup a breeze and mealtime a pleasure

- 50 of the best fast, healthy recipes mouth-watering recipes that will have you and your family begging for seconds

THIS BOOK IS NOT:

- A hodge-podge of all the recipes in the known universe so large it just confuses you;
- A guilt trip to steer you away from the foods you love;
- A weight-reducing program (though it won't load you up with too many diet-busters);
- A push to save time with convenience foods loaded with more chemicals than the periodic table in an effort to save time in the kitchen.

THIS BOOK IS:

- A cooking and eating plan that simply uses natural, unprocessed ingredients and no-fuss cooking techniques;
- A collection of 50 easy and delicious recipes everyone will love to give your body sound nutrition, your taste buds a pleasure fest and get you out of the kitchen as fast as possible;
- The smart, modern approach to eating for everyone who wants delicious, healthful food, with a minimum of work, even if you never have to worry about the numbers on your scale.

WHAT DID YOU HAVE FOR YOUR LAST TEN MEALS?

Cooking is more than a list of ingredients, gadgets and techniques. It is a philosophy.

My philosophy is that life is too short not to eat well, every time we sit down to a meal.

Yet, a study done some years ago revealed that most families eat the same ten dishes year in and year out. Quite astounding really, when there are thousands of recipes available from every region of the world, enough to provide a different delicacy at every meal for an entire lifetime.

Think about *your* last ten meals. Was every dish a surprise--exciting and delicious? Or did you fall into the "same old ten dinners" rut?

If the food you like takes too much time to prepare, or you don't have the energy at the end of the day to spend hours coming up with something new, or you think healthy is boring, difficult or too expensive, they probably were. **How To Cook Healthy in a Hurry** will change all that.

THESE RECIPES ARE FOR EVERYBODY

Whether you need kid-friendly dishes like tacos and burgers or elegant date-night specials like steak with wine sauce, you will find dishes that will please singles and families, adults and kids, people who eat to live and those of us who live to eat. But wait. There's more.

You've heard the expression, give a man a fish and he will eat for a day, teach him to fish and he will eat for a lifetime.

So you won't just get delicious recipes for crowd-pleasers such as:

Best Black Bean Chili
Chicken Parmesan
Cherry Pistachio Crisps

14

You will find a mini-cooking course here; all the secrets to cooking, shopping and planning your kitchen that will help you improve all your meals. From now on you will be able to cook and shop smarter healthier and faster. So let's get cooking.

WHAT DOES IT MEAN TO COOK HEALTHY IN A HURRY

Healthy nutrition simply means making wise choices. Learning to read labels to avoid additives that are known health risks. Opting for fresh, seasonal, pesticide-free produce. Buying wild fish and free range meat and poultry that are not raised on diets loaded with antibiotics and other chemicals that can harm us.

But healthy and SMART nutrition also means using those nifty kitchen helpers that will aid in getting dinner on the table without pulling out every pot and pan in your kitchen. Healthy in a Hurry encourages you to speed up dinner time by taking advantage of commercial sauces, condiments, frozen vegetables and rice, canned fruits and sauces that are as healthy as if you had made them from scratch.

THE 80-20 RULE: OR PEOPLE WHO WALK DOWN THE MIDDLE OF THE ROAD GET HIT FROM BOTH SIDES

Healthy eating is not about achieving perfection or never veering from a 100% healthful, organic, pesticide and chemical free diet. It is about making wise choices and balance. When you want to indulge in a salty, crispy, fatty, sugary treats with ingredients not found in nature, go ahead. Enjoy, as long as you follow the 80-20 rule.

In many areas of life we are discovering the 80-20 rule. It seems to be a law of the universe. In business, for example, it is often true that 80% of effort produces 20% of return.

In healthful cooking, *assuming you have no dietary restrictions*, if you follow health-conscious guidelines 80%

16

of the time, then approximately 20% of the time you can stray from the program—whatever your nutritional commitment is—and still achieve your goals. That means the bulk of your meals will have lots of fresh, pesticide-free produce, whole grains, fish, lean meat and poultry. Most meals will shy away from excessive sugar, fats and overly processed foods like white flour, snacks and convenience foods. But you can also splurge from time to time guilt-free.

Therefore, with the 80-20 rule, you will find in this book some yummy, calorie intensive recipes that use bacon, cheese, cream, sugar and other ingredients the diet police tell us to avoid. But when these ingredients are used in moderation in a recipe (such an ugly word but oh it makes so much sense), they add plate appeal, taste appeal and can offer cooking shortcuts.

Just keep the treats at approximately 20% of your total intake and the good-for-you stuff a whopping 80% of your meals. That's all. No counting calories, carbs or grams (unless your doctor tells you to). Use common sense and eyeball what you're eating.

The 80-20 rule allows you to balance your diet the healthy, easy way, without relentless counting of fat and calories.

So let's get started.

HOW TO READ A RECIPE

We make a big mistake when we assume that just because a recipe is short, the dish will be easy. Consider this recipe for a roast chicken from an 18th century cookery book, back when recipes were called receipts.

Wring neck of chicken, pluck it, clean it and roast it on a spit until done.

Yes, the whole recipe is just one sentence long. But it would take me all day just to work up my nerve to catch a live chicken.

On the other hand, many cooks shy away from a recipe that covers a page or two, thinking it will take hours to prepare. However, the time it takes to go from stove to dinner table may only be 15 or 20 minutes, but the thoughtful recipe writer has included all the hints, tips and tricks you need to make it foolproof. Taking a minute or two read a lengthy recipe could improve your knowledge every time you cook, even if you are an experienced chef. There is always some new trick to learn, without necessarily adding to your time in the kitchen.

However, some recipe writers condense recipes to make them look easy by enticing you with just a few instructions. Unfortunately, many of these so-called quickies can leave out important information and leave you wondering why the dish didn't turn out as described. Don't let this type of short recipe dampen your enthusiasm for cooking and make you doubt your skills because it didn't work. Here are a few recipe-reading tricks to help you plan your menus.

YOU ARE THE MASTER OF YOUR KITCHEN: DON'T BE A SLAVE TO A RECIPE

First of all, remember that it is your kitchen, your mealtime. No recipe, even if it comes from the most celebrated chef or restaurant, will flavor all dishes to please all diners. Over time, we develop our own preferred tastes and techniques. When a recipe instructs you to season to taste, it means just that. Add seasonings so that the dish makes you happy, even if it means eliminating the garlic or adding more ginger or experimenting with herbs where none are called for in the recipe. If you have invented a trick to make a recipe easier or tastier, whether in this book or any other, use it.

When a recipe goes wrong, is it your fault or the recipe writer's? Sadly, not every recipe published in books or on line is tested, unless it is from a reputable blogger, cooking magazine, publisher or cookbook like this one. Sometimes very good cooks are not very good at documenting their recipes. Steps and ingredients get left out or the timing isn't accurate.

They might be like my Aunt Nellie who took the best recipes I've ever tasted for shortbread and batter fried fish with her to the grave. When I asked how to make them, she said, oh just put some flour and shortening in a bowl and mix it. Huh?

If you followed all the instructions to the letter and the dish was just a half a turn off, it could be because your stove or cookware had different heating properties or the ingredients and brands you used were not exactly like the writer's. Be prepared to make minor adjustments to a recipe, but if it is a disaster, move on to something else.

When choosing a recipe to beat the clock, consider these points:

- Cooking time isn't always an indication of the relative ease or difficulty of a recipe. Look at the number of steps involved and the time each takes. A stir-fry recipe may cook quickly at the last minute.

However, you may not have enough time to chop all the meats and vegetables and prepare all the sauces beforehand. On the other hand, a roast chicken takes up to two hours depending on the size and method, but only minutes to get it into the oven.

- Be sure you understand the cooking times for all the steps.

- Check if you can prepare things simultaneously. While your vegetables are browning or the chicken is marinating, can you prepare a salad or put a glaze together for the entrée? If you have to devote all your time to one dish, as for deep-frying for instance, chances are you won't get dinner on the table in less than 30 minutes.

- If you have a long list of ingredients, do they have to be prepped or cooked separately? Or can you just put them in the pot and let them simmer?

- Is there a way that you know that will streamline the dish or perk up the flavor to suit you and your family's tastes?

As someone once said, be fearless when you dance, and I would also add, be fearless you cook. You won't hurt my feelings if you use these recipes as a jumping off place to create your own versions that ultimately delights you and your family.

FIGHT FEAR OF RECIPES WITH THE HEALTHY IN A HURRY COOKING PLAN

Mealtime can find us scattered from the day, struggling to switch gears from work to hearth. Hmm, you think, scanning a recipe, where do I start?

The Healthy in a Hurry Cooking Plan is your roadmap to the dinner table. This brief guide shows you where to start and where to finish. Even if a recipe is dense with important information that takes up many paragraphs, this ingenious aid outlines the steps to follow up front, so you can see at glance how to proceed with each recipe and how long it will take.

THE HERE'S A TIP FEATURE

In addition to the Cooking Plan and detailed instructions, Healthy in A Hurry points out labor or money saving tips and tricks. You will find them listed under "Here's A Tip" rather than buried in the recipe for you to figure out on your own. These tips will enhance your skills and all of your meals.

UP AGAINST THE WALL, SHOPPERS

Supermarket designers have made healthful shopping easy. When you enter your favorite market, head for the walls. That is where the supers stock the produce, dairy, fish and meat, the fresh, unprocessed, chemical-free, seasonal items you want for most of your meals.

Tread carefully around center aisles where the processed, pretend food lives. You know, the boxes and cans that contain more items from the Periodic Table than the vegetable garden.

Healthful shopping means that your ancestors would recognize the meal you put in front of them. It will contain fresh, sustainable produce, fish, meat and dairy with a minimum of ingredients you have to look up in a dictionary to know what they are.

Choose as many organic, pesticide-free fruits and vegetables as possible. Pick free-range beef and poultry, and avoid farmed fish in favor of ocean-caught with sustainable fishing practices.

When you do use flavor intensifiers and kitchen helpers out of a box, jar or can, make sure they follow the same rule—they should have real food ingredients with no or minimal additives, excessive high fructose corn syrups and other sweeteners or hydrogenated or partially-hydrogenated oils—the ones that turn healthy fats into artery busters. Make reading labels your mantra so you always know what you and your loved ones are consuming.

HOW TO READ A FOOD LABEL

Federal law requires all packaged foods to have labels that include nutritional information by weight. The first five ingredients listed have the largest volume. Think of the 80-20 rule. If there are too many chemicals—the words you can't pronounce—in those first five ingredients, choose something else. Processed foods did not become popular until after WW2. If you would have to explain to a farmer from the 1920's what's in a package, you should probably make another selection.

Not all additives are harmful. Citrates, for example, are often packed in tomatoes and won't harm you. If you have a sensitive palate though, you might taste this preservative. You will find pectin in preserves as thickening agents that are perfectly fine. Deciphering labels as a step to good nutrition is a learning process, one well worth the effort. Let technology help you. Scan the Internet for sites on nutrition and to help you identify puzzling ingredients.

By all means, use kitchen helpers that come in cans and packages, such as broths, tomato sauces and frozen items. Many producers are on the bandwagon supplying us with healthful convenience foods. Markets such as Trader Joe's and Whole Foods specialize in these items. Dress up fresh, seasonal produce, meats, fish and poultry with flavor intensive commercial glazes, dressings, sauces and condiments. You will find many products available in supermarkets and online that will make your busy life easier, spark up your meals and leave you with some energy to spare to enjoy your evening with family and friends. Just read the labels before you buy.

BEST HEALTHY IN A HURRY COOKING METHODS

While we love slow braised short ribs and mouthwatering tender stews that simmer for hours, they aren't the dishes you throw together after a busy day at work. By all means, enjoy these dishes, but save labor-intensive recipes for a weekend or special occasions. How do you know the difference? Here are some guidelines

Choose Recipes That Call For These Quick-Cooking Methods

Sautéing
Broiling
Steaming
Pan Frying
Grilling
Poaching

Avoid These Slow-Cooking Methods

Braising
Roasting meats and whole poultry
Long marinating times
Stews
Brining
Deep-frying

THE HEALTHY IN A HURRY PANTRY

A well-stocked pantry is the secret to great Healthy in a Hurry meals. With a good supply of staples and kitchen helpers on hand, you don't have to make last minute runs to the supermarket, or use second rate substitutions because you have run out of a key ingredient.

Here is a suggested list of items to keep on hand to help you create the recipes that follow. It is by no means a complete list of must haves, but it is a start. Add to it as you experiment with interesting products that suit your and your diners' tastes.

Have On Hand In The Refrigerator:

Note: use organic dairy products and cage-free eggs; use pesticide-free produce, especially for items without a skin you would peel and discard; use grass-fed beef and free-range poultry

Butter
Lower fat and calorie butter-like spreads made from
    yogurt and healthy oils
Milk
Plain yogurt
Light sour cream
Onions
Garlic
Baby carrots
Red peppers
Greens
Chemical-free bacon, pancetta and low fat sausages
Relishes, bottled chutneys and savory spreads, such
    as olive tapenade
Lemons and limes
Parmesan and other favorite cheeses
Fresh herbs such as parsley, cilantro and basil

Have On Hand In The Cupboard:

Variety of pastas
Canned tuna, salmon and clams
Bottled clam juice
Chicken, beef and vegetable broth (try Better Than
    Bouillon)
Refried, white and other canned beans
Asian fish sauce
Hoisin sauce
Soy sauce
Hot sauce
Canned fruit without excessive sugar
Mandarin oranges and apple sauce
Raisins and other dried fruits
Nuts
Bread crumbs and bread cubes
Tortillas, corn, wheat and whole wheat
Crusty, home style breads

Oils and vinegars
Dried herbs and spices, seasoning and spice blends
    for meat, chicken and fish, such as fajita
    seasoning and lemon pepper

TOOLS OF THE TRADE

It is true that many hands make light work, but so will a wisely collected assortment of kitchen gear. I have a weakness for gourmet food shops and kitchenware stores and my cupboards and drawers overflow with cherry pitters, shrimp deveiners and pineapple corers I never use. But the items I cannot live without and which I recommend all cooks have, make life in the kitchen easier and cooking more fun. The other toys you can acquire at will.

Here is a tip for budget-minded cooks when you are tricking out your kitchen for minimum mealtime fuss. Scour second-hand shops, Craigslist and e-bay for used but high quality kitchen equipment. Many of these appliances and high-end cookware items never wear out.

My first ricer (see below) cost $.25 when I set up my kitchen as a young bride. I used it for years and years until the red enamel started to flake off the handle. My cast iron skillets (I have three different sizes) came from the same Salvation Army shop and were about a dollar each back then. I'm still using them.

I have a number of All Clad pots that I was able to get on eBay for half the price of new ones. Sometimes you can find seconds that are as good as what you would find in a gourmet shop. Also scour discount stores, such as Home Goods and Ross for Less. If you can save money on used or auction items, you might be able to splurge on a high quality food processor or blender.

Make a kitchenware wish list for holiday and birthdays and slip it to your beloveds. Here are some items you might want to include.

Food Saver™

I constantly sing the praises of this gadget that vacuum packs food items and leftovers for freezing, giving me an assortment of ingredients to choose from when I'm on the go.

If I see steak or salmon on sale at my market, for instance, I stock up, then cut them into individual portions, vacuum pack and freeze. They thaw quickly and save a trip to the market.

Immersion or Stick Blender

This ingenious device allows you to puree soups and vegetables without having to transfer foods from pot to blender and back again, piling up dirty dishes in the sink. You can't completely replace your blender, but when you're racing the clock, reach for the stick and process your food in the pot.

Milk Frother

Battery operated and resembling a pint-sized immersion blender, this little gadget solves the dilemma of putting a thick foam of milk on homemade coffee. Whisk your hot milk and dress up your morning cuppa to look like a latte or cappuccino. However, also I find a frother invaluable for whisking salad dressings and small batches of sauces.

Microplane Grater™

I've heard some people say that if they were stuck on a desert island the one thing they would want with them is their Microplane™ grater. Frankly, I'd opt for an unlimited supply of fresh water and a box of flares, but I get the point. The Microplane is unparalleled for grating zest (outer skin of citrus fruit), chocolate and cheese. You can't imagine the kick this gadget will give to your food when you discover how easy it is to perk up a soup or salad with uniform flakes of orange or lemon peel or some fragrant, fresh cheese.

Easy Care Cookware

It took me a while to accumulate my collection of pots and pans but I have never regretted plunging hard-earned cash into my All-Clad™, Emile Henry™, and Le Creuset™, cookware. You may find other brands you prefer, but even if you can afford only one piece a year, opt for a brand that provides even cooking and easy to clean surfaces. You will treasure this investment for a lifetime.

Cast Iron Skillets

I have had mine for my entire cooking life. Buy them in several sizes for making cornbread, sautéing vegetables, bacon and other meats. These skillets produce perfectly cooked burgers, steaks and eggs, among other dishes. An added bonus is that they can go from stovetop to oven to finish up a dish.

Hand Mixer

By all means put a Kitchen Aid™ Stand Mixer on your wish list. I've had mine for 35 years and it has served me through recipe testing for several cookbooks, numerous cooking classes and countless parties. But a really good hand mixer will save the day when you need to whip some cream or an egg white or two in a hurry.

Food Processor

How did we get dinner on the table before the food processor was invented? Certainly not as quickly. There are many makes and models. Choose one that will fit your budget, and, if you are not counting your pennies, buy a large bowl processor and a mini processor for quick chopping and mincing chores. And here is possibly the best tip for using your processor. KEEP IT ON THE COUNTER. Cooks forego using some of their laborsaving devices because they store them out of sight and don't want the hassle of dragging them out. IN SIGHT/IN USE is my motto.

Potato Ricer

I depend on the ricer for squeezing dry cooked spinach and producing perfectly mashed potatoes. Many of my students have never heard of a potato ricer. However, you should see their ecstatic faces when the finally invest in one (they only cost a few dollars).

Potato Roaster

This covered, unglazed clay pot will amaze you as you stick potatoes, sea salt and maybe a few herbs inside and pop it into the oven. The result is potatoes that are creamy, sweet and tender and need no additional butter or cream. The easiest and most spectacular kitchen trick I know.

Now let's get on to The Recipes.

APPETIZERS

You never want to spoil anybody's appetite with hefty snacks just before dinner is ready. But you can't blame your beloveds for succumbing to the tantalizing smells coming from the kitchen that sends them begging for a treat. So give them one of these five quick, delectable snacks to calm them down before the main event.

Mango Salsa Toast

Melba toast
3-4 tablespoons queso cotija, queso fresca or other
    tangy Mexican cheese
½ cup fresh commercial mango salsa
Sprigs of fresh cilantro

Spread Melba toasts with cheese, salsa and top with a sprig
of cilantro before serving.

Quick Guacamole

2 avocados, peeled, pitted and coarsely mashed
1/2 cup fresh or commercial salsa
2 tablespoons lime juice or to taste
2 tablespoons chopped cilantro
Salt and hot sauce to taste
Tortilla chips, pita chips, celery or carrot sticks

Blend first five ingredients and serve with the chips and
sticks.

Feta and Olive Bruschetta

1/2 cup crumbled feta cheese, plain or with
    Mediterranean herbs
2 tablespoons whole milk or enough to thin the
    cheese to a smooth consistency
Leaves from 3 to 4 sprigs oregano

Black pepper to taste
3 tablespoons pitted, chopped Kalamata olives
Thin slices of French bread

Blend feta, milk, oregano and pepper in a food processor
and serve on French bread.

Beans and Salsa on Chips

1/4 cup fat-free, vegetarian canned refried beans
Tortilla chips
3 tablespoons salsa
1 1/2 teaspoons finely chopped fresh cilantro

Heat the beans in the microwave for 10 seconds. Exact time
will depend on the power of your oven Spoon onto the
tortilla chips and add salsa and cilantro. Serve immediately.

Celery, Peanut Butter and Cream Cheese Sticks

Layer celery sticks with peanut butter and cream cheese
and serve.

SOUPS

Soups are the kitchen gods' gift to the harried cook. Whether you quickly puree left over vegetables with broth or cream to take the edge off appetites before dinner, or bulk them up with meat, fish, beans and seasonings for a one-dish extravaganza, think soup when you want to get a meal on the table in a hurry. Here are some ideas to whet your appetite.

Easy Tortilla and Bean Soup

Hearty, filling and delicious, those adjectives would be enough to induce any cook to try this soup. But with the added inducement of speed and ease, this will soon become a favorite. Be sure that you use canned vegetarian refried beans to cut down on the saturated fat.

COOKING PLAN: Cook bacon and vegetables, add remaining ingredients, simmer, season and serve. Note: Don't microwave the bacon—you want some of the fat in the pan to season the soup.

> 2 strips Applewood or other artisan bacon
> 1 tablespoon olive oil
> ¼ cup minced celery
> ¼ cup minced onion
> 1 can low-fat or vegetarian refried beans
> 1 cup chicken broth, or more for desired
>   consistency
> 3 tablespoons canned, diced chilies or to taste
> ½ cup light sour cream or plain yogurt
> 1/2 cup shredded Cheddar or Monterey Jack cheese
>   or combination, more if desired
> 1/2 cup tortilla chips, crumbled, more if desired

In a heavy bottomed saucepan, cook the bacon over medium high heat until crisp. Remove the bacon to a paper towel to drain excess fat. Discard all but one tablespoon of the bacon fat from the pan.

Add the olive oil to the bacon fat and heat until the oil is just smoking but not burning. Add the celery and stir until softened, 2-3 minutes.

Add the beans, chicken broth and diced chilies. Bring to a boil and stir until smooth. Reduce the heat and simmer for 5 minutes or until very hot.

Serve hot in bowls with a dollop of sour cream or yogurt, the cheese and tortilla chips.

Serves 4

Carrot, Apple and Ginger Soup

"Baby" carrots, those packages of two-inch long nubs, relieve you of the chore of peeling and chopping their big sisters. Of course, they aren't really babies at all, but regular carrots peeled down to the sweet centers for nibbling, or tossing into the saucepan for soup.

HERE'S A TIP: When prepping the apples, cut them in half and place them on one side and slice away the core. Then just peel them. Faster than trying to peel a whole apple.

COOKING PLAN: Cook the shallots, add remaining ingredients and cook until carrots are tender. Puree and serve.

1 tablespoon canola or grapeseed oil
2 shallots, peeled and coarsely chopped
1 small Gaia or Fuji apple, or other tart green apple, halved, peeled and cored
1 pound baby carrots
3 cups chicken broth
½ teaspoon ground ginger or to taste
Pinch of brown sugar or to taste
1/2 cup half and half or milk, more if desired
Heat the oil in a large saucepan until just smoking and add the shallots. Reduce the heat to medium and stir for two minutes or until softened.

Add the apple, carrots, broth, ginger and sugar and bring to a boil, stirring frequently. Reduce the heat to medium and cook for 15 minutes or until the carrots are tender.

Stir in the half and half. With an immersion blender, puree the soup until smooth. Taste for seasoning, adding more ginger or sugar as desired. Serve hot.

Serves 4

Best Black Bean Chili

Why is this the best black bean chili? Because it is delicious, healthful and comes together in a snap.

HERE'S A TIP: This recipe calls for nonfat yogurt as a topping to curb the fat, but you can substitute light or full fat sour cream if you desire. Or, blend half nonfat yogurt with sour cream for a richer taste while still curbing fat and calories if needed.

COOKING PLAN: Simmer first nine ingredients, add corn and stir until heated, serve with cilantro and toppings.

> 2 cans black beans and their liquid
> ½ small onion, coarsely chopped
> 1 small carrot, coarsely chopped
> 1 garlic clove, minced
> 1 teaspoon ground cumin
> ¼ teaspoon ground cinnamon
> Pinch each of dried oregano and dried thyme
> ½ cup canned diced tomatoes
> Salt and pepper
> 1 cup frozen corn
> ¼ cup minced, fresh cilantro
> ¾ cup nonfat plain yogurt (see note above about substituting sour cream)
> Fresh salsa if desired

Place the beans and their liquid, onion, carrot, garlic, cumin, cinnamon, oregano, thyme and tomatoes in a large saucepan and bring to a boil. Reduce the heat and simmer for 15 minutes or until onions and carrots are tender.

Season with salt and pepper to taste. Add the corn, stir and cook for 3 minutes. Serve hot with a sprinkle of cilantro, a dollop of yogurt and a spoonful of salsa.

Serves 4

Tortellini Minestrone

Here we have another meal in a bowl made from healthful items you can grab from your pantry and freezer. To this quick, nutritious, delicious soup, add a crisp salad and crusty bread to soak up the juices and presto, you have dinner. Note: if you use fresh tortellini, cut down on the cooking time or it will be mushy. Add the tortellini according to the directions on the package, a few minutes AFTER you add the vegetables.

COOKING PLAN*: Microwave bacon, cook onions. Heat with beans, broth and tomatoes, add remaining ingredients and serve.*

> 2 strips microwaved Applewood or other artisan
>   bacon, set aside on paper towels to drain
> 1 tablespoon olive oil
> ¼ cup diced onion
> 1 clove minced garlic
> 1 cup canned white beans, rinsed and drained
> 3 cups chicken broth
> 1 14/1/2-ounce can diced tomatoes with liquid
> 1 16-ounce package of frozen Italian vegetables
> 8 ounces frozen spinach tortellini
> ½ cup grated Parmesan cheese

Heat the olive oil until just steaming in a Dutch oven or other heavy-bottomed pot. Do not let the oil brown or burn. Add onion and garlic and stir for 4-5 minutes or until the onion is softened but not brown.

Add white beans, chicken broth, tomatoes and their liquid and bring to a boil. Reduce heat and simmer for 3 minutes.

With immersion blender, beat to a coarse puree in the pot.

Add the vegetables and tortellini and bring to a boil. Reduce the heat to a simmer and cook for 10 minutes or until vegetables are tender but not mushy. Crumble the bacon over the soup and serve hot with a sprinkle of Parmesan cheese.

Serves 4

Potato and Bacon Chowder

Make this quick star-studded soup as lean or rich as you wish by choosing milk or cream. When you are not challenging the clock, sauté the leeks, celery, carrots and pepper in 2 tablespoons of olive oil for a deeper flavor.

HERE'S A TIP: If you wish a more elegant presentation for a party, before you add the corn and bacon, puree the soup in a blender or with an immersion blender. However, NEVER put cooked potatoes in a food processor or you will have a bowl of library paste on your hands. Also, do not use waxy boiling potatoes, because they do not have enough starch to make a creamy soup.

COOKING PLAN*: Cook the vegetables in broth until tender, puree with milk or cream. Stir in corn and serve.*

>3 slices microwaved Applewood or other artisan
>   bacon, drained on paper towels and set aside
>4 cups chicken broth
>3 large Russet or Idaho potatoes, peeled and diced
>   in 1 inch cubes
>2 leeks, washed and sliced, white part only
>½ cup diced celery
>½ cup diced carrots
>½ red pepper, diced
>1 cup milk, half and half or cream
>1 cup corn niblets

Bring the chicken broth to a boil, reduce the heat to medium and add the potatoes, leeks, celery, carrots and red pepper. Cook until the vegetables are tender, about 15-20 minutes, depending on size of potatoes.

Add the milk and corn and cook until heated through. Season to taste with salt and pepper.

Garnish with the crumbled bacon and serve immediately.

Serves 4

Tomato and Bread Soup

What could be easier than turning a leftover loaf of crusty bread and a can of tomatoes into a meal? I like this classic soup mid-winter with organic canned tomatoes, or mid-summer with Heirlooms from the farmer's market or the backyard vegetable patch. The quick version here calls for canned tomatoes, but for fresh tomatoes, simply chop them coarsely and add to the pot, juice and all. Serve with a salad and a rotisserie chicken from your local market for an easy meal.

COOKING PLAN: *Toast the bread. Sauté garlic and onion, add bread, tomatoes, broth and herbs and cook for 15 minutes. Serve with cheese.*

Preheat oven to 350 degrees F.

> 4 large slices stale crusty bread, such as French or Italian, sliced
> 2 tablespoons olive oil
> 1 clove garlic, minced
> ½ red onion, chopped
> 1 12-ounce can diced tomatoes
> Salt and pepper to taste
> 3 cups chicken broth
> 3 tablespoons chopped fresh Italian parsley
> 3 tablespoons chopped fresh basil
> 1/4 cup grated Parmesan cheese, more if desired

Toast the bread until is a deep golden brown but not scorched. Because it is already a day or so old, it will be hard when you take it out of the toaster, which is desirable. Set aside.

Heat the olive oil in a large saucepan over medium heat. Do not allow it to smoke. Stir in the garlic and onion. Stir over

44

medium heat until the onion has softened, about 5 minutes. Do not allow the onion to brown.

Add the tomatoes, salt, pepper, chicken broth, parsley and basil. Raise the heat to a boil and immediately reduce the heat to a simmer. Continue to simmer for 15 minutes or until the tomatoes are soft and the flavors are blended. Taste for seasoning, adding more basil if necessary. Crumble in the toasted bread and stir until the bread disintegrates, another 4-5 minutes. Serve in bowls garnished with the cheese.

Serves 4

FISH

No one disputes the healthful properties of fish. All those great omega thingies protecting our arteries and keeping strokes and heart attacks at bay. But fish is also the hurried cook's BFF. You can't beat the bounty from the sea for variety, flavor and ease of cooking. In fact, if you cook fish too long it turns rubbery and tasteless. Whether you want to add it to a vegetable medley for a quick, hearty fish chowder or sauté thin slivers briefly with lemon and capers for an instant elegant entrée, keep fish recipes at top of your list for mealtime success.

Linguini with Clams and Garlic

By all means, if you live near a fishery use fresh clams when they are in season for this succulent, fast and easy one-dish meal. But don't scoff at the canned variety. They have their own sea-kissed charm.

HERE'S A TIP: If you are not familiar with cooking pasta, put the Parmesan away because you never serve cheese with a fish pasta.

COOKING PLAN: Cook the pasta. Sauté the garlic and onion, add the clams and herbs and when hot pour over pasta and serve.

> 1 pound linguini
> 1 tablespoon extra virgin olive oil
> ½ cup mixed Italian and leafy parsley, minced and
>   set aside
> 4 tablespoons butter
> 1 medium onion, diced
> 3 cloves garlic, peeled and minced
> 2 6-ounce cans minced clams and their liquid
> Salt and pepper to taste

Cook the linguini in salted boiling water until al dente, about 7 minutes. Drain and return to the sauce pan and stir in 1 tablespoon olive oil so the pasta doesn't congeal while you prepare the sauce.

While the pasta is cooking, heat the butter in a large skillet over medium heat and add the onion and garlic. Stir over medium heat until softened but not brown, about 4-5 minutes.

Stir in the clams and their liquid. Bring to a boil, then reduce the heat to a simmer and cook until the sauce is heated through, no more than 3-5 minutes.

Add the cooked linguini and parsley, stir until the noodles are thoroughly coated with the clam sauce, season with salt and pepper if desired and serve immediately.

Serves 4

Tuna and White Bean Wraps

Don't shy away from the list of ingredients in this no-cook package of flavor, texture and taste. It goes from zero to 60 in the time it takes to set the table. Basically a Dagwood Bumsted-style sandwich (look up the old Blondie comics), these wraps are filled with heart-healthy Mediterranean flavors and Mexican-inspired quick preparation. Use this recipe as a starting point and add more or fewer flavorings to suit your taste.

COOKING PLAN: *Blend all ingredients except spinach in a bowl. Spoon into tortillas and serve.*

> 1 5-ounce can tuna, drained (I prefer packed in olive oil but water packed will work also)
> 1 15-ounce can white beans, drained and rinsed
> 1 fresh tomato, seeded and diced
> 1/2 large cucumber, peeled, seeded and diced
> 3 green onions, chopped, white part only
> 1/4 cup Italian or leafy parsley, finely chopped
> Hot sauce to taste if desired
> ¼ cup pitted and coarsely chopped black or green olives
> 2 tablespoons olive oil
> 1 tablespoon red wine vinegar
> Salt and freshly ground black pepper
> 1 teaspoon fresh lemon juice
> 2 ounces baby spinach or mixed greens
> 5 large whole wheat tortillas

In a mixing bowl add all the ingredients except the spinach and tortillas. Break up the tuna with a fork and mix well.

Season to taste with salt and pepper, adjusting the ingredients to your preference and blend once more.

Place the tortillas on plates and dividing equally, add one layer of the greens and top with the tuna mix. Fold in thirds and serve.

Serves 4

Cherry Glazed Prawns with Forbidden Black Rice

If you haven't sampled black, also known as forbidden, rice, look for the small ebony grains packaged by, among other brands, Lotus Foods. They contain the same antioxidant as those healthful powerhouses, blueberries and acai berries.

Legend has it that this rice, like Emperor Tea, was reserved for the royals in China. But now everyone can enjoy this easy-to-cook, surprisingly sweet grain. It turns a deep purple when cooked and is both breathtaking and mouth-watering when paired with rich, pink cherry-glazed prawns.

HERE'S A TIP: If you can't find black rice, substitute my new favorite discovery, frozen, cooked brown rice that just needs a few minutes in the microwave before serving. A bowl of steamed broccoli or broccoli rabe would make a picture-perfect menu.

HERE'S ANOTHER TIP: Buy prawns that are already peeled and deveined A little more expensive but worth the timesaving factor.

COOKING PLAN: Steam black rice (takes 30 minutes) and while it cooks, prepare glaze for prawns. Sauté prawns, brush with glaze and serve with the black rice.

1 cup black rice
1 ¾ cup water
Pinch of salt

1/3 cup cherry preserves

1 teaspoon red wine vinegar
2 tablespoons water to thin the preserves

1 tablespoon olive oil
1 pound prawns, peeled and deveined

Place the rice, water and salt in a covered saucepan. Bring to a boil, cover and reduce the heat to a simmer. Cook for 30 minutes. Remove from the heat and let stand for several minutes before removing the lid. Fluff and serve.

Meanwhile, stir the cherry preserves, red wine vinegar and water (just enough to make a pourable glaze) in a microwaveable bowl. Microwave for 20 seconds or until steaming. Exact time will depend on the power of your oven. Set aside.

Seven minutes before serving, heat a heavy bottomed skillet and add the olive oil. When it is hot but not burning, add the prawns. Cook on each side for 3-4 minutes or just until they turn pink. Do not overcook.

Coat the prawns with the cherry glaze during the last minute of cooking and serve with the black rice.

Serves 4

Fish Tacos

Anything wrapped in a warmed corn tortilla and flavored with spices, cream and slaw has me by the taste buds. See if you don't agree with these scrumptious tacos, a Latin version of a fish sandwich. You may find the recipe reads long, but the cooking is easy and quick.

HERE'S A TIP: You can prepare the fish the morning or night before and reheat in the microwave with a few tablespoons of water. You can also use commercial taco seasoning. And do try oranges or tangerines with your toppings. They have a wonderful, mellowing effect on spicy food. And always cook fish 10 minutes per inch of thickness.

COOKING PLAN: Prepare onions in vinegar ahead of time. Marinate fish (can be done ahead). Cook fish and serve with toppings.

Marinated Red Onions (recipe follows)
1/4 cup olive oil
1 1/2 teaspoons ancho chili powder
1 1/2 teaspoons dried oregano
1/2 teaspoon ground cumin
1/4 cup lightly packed fresh cilantro leaves,
    chopped, plus more for garnish
1 Jalapeño, stemmed and chopped, optional
1 pound flaky white fish (such as mahi mahi or
    cod), cut into 4 pieces
Salt
8 fresh corn tortillas

Into a baking dish large enough to hold the fish in one layer, add the olive oil, ancho chili powder, oregano, cumin, chopped cilantro, and jalapeño if you are using it. Blend thoroughly. Add the fish and turn on both sides so it is completely covered with the marinade. Set aside for 15-20 minutes.

Just before serving, heat the olive oil in a skillet over medium-high heat. Add the fish, shaking it to remove the excess marinade. Salt lightly and cook for 4 minutes, turn, and continue cooking for 2 minutes more or until the fish is cooked through but not overdone. Remove to a serving dish.

While the fish cooks, place the tortillas between two damp paper towels, set on a microwavable plate and cook on high for 45 seconds. Exact time will depend on the power of your oven. You may need to do this in two batches.

Onto each warm tortilla, spoon the fish and marinated onions. Add the toppings and serve with the remaining lime quarters and cilantro.

Serves 4

Choose one or more of these suggested toppings:

>2 Mandarin oranges or tangerines, peeled and
>   separated into segments or canned
>½ cup deli coleslaw
>Mexican crema, homemade or commercial, or light
>   sour cream thinned with 1-2 tablespoons milk
>Queso fresca or feta cheese
>Fresh (not bottled) salsa, commercial or homemade
>
>2 limes, cut into quarters
>Handful of cilantro sprigs

Marinated Red Onions

The marinated onions keep for a week or more covered in the refrigerator. However, they may not last that long as you realize how well they spark up fish dishes, sandwiches and burgers. So the prep time for them is really an investment in a quick, flavorful punch for many other dishes.

>1/2 red onion, thinly sliced
>1 1/2 cups red wine or raspberry vinegar
>2 teaspoons sugar

Place the sliced onion in a covered container and add the vinegar and sugar and blend well. Allow to sit for half an hour or, if you wish to prepare it ahead, refrigerate until needed in a tightly covered container for up to two weeks.

Oven-Roasted Cod Nicoise

Inspired by the cuisine of Nice in the south of France, this easy one dish meal is easy and flavorful.

HERE'S A TIP: Use leftover boiled potatoes if you have them.

HERE'S ANOTHER TIP: Fish cooks for approximately 10 minutes per inch of thickness. Use this measurement to gauge your cooking time, regardless of what any recipe will tell you.

COOKING PLAN: Steam potatoes. Add to roasting pan with all ingredients except fish. Cook in oven until done, add fish, cook another few minutes and serve.

Preheat oven to 425 degrees F.

1 pound small, red spring potatoes, halved and
    microwaved for 5 minutes or until barely tender.
    Exact time will depend on the power of your
    oven (they will continue to cook with the fish)
1 pound green beans, ends trimmed
4 fresh tomatoes, chopped
2 cloves of garlic, peeled and crushed
Salt and pepper to taste
3 tablespoons fresh oregano, minced
3 tablespoons fresh parsley, minced
¼ cup olive oil
½ cup dry white wine
¼ cup pitted black or green olives
4 fillets of cod, halibut or other firm fleshed fish

Arrange the cooked potatoes, beans, tomatoes and garlic on the bottom of a heavy bottomed roasting pan.

Season with salt and pepper and drizzle the olive oil and wine over the vegetables and stir, coating everything with the oil. Roast for 5 minutes or until the beans are bright green, slightly tender but not mushy.

Stir in the herbs and olives and arrange the fish over the vegetables. Spoon the liquid over the fish to coat it completely. Return to the oven to cook for approximately 7 minutes or until the fish is firm and white in the center but not falling apart. Do not overcook. Season to taste with salt and pepper and serve immediately.

Serves 4

Poached Salmon with Pesto

Poaching, that is, simmering fish in a flavorful liquid, produces perfectly cooked and seasoned salmon. Traditionally, cooks plopped the fish into a long, covered fish poacher (I have two, but then that's me and cooking toys), but any covered saucepan or skillet large enough to hold the fish in one layer will do. The advantage of a poacher is that it has a rack that makes retrieving the fish from the poaching liquid easy.

HERE'S A TIP: If you are not familiar with bouquet garni (an herb packet of parsley, bay leaf and thyme for starters used in soups, stews and poaching liquids), look for them pre-packaged and wrapped in cheesecloth in gourmet shops or online. However, you can make your own by placing the herbs and spices inside a bunch of parsley and wrapping it in cheesecloth yourself or just tie up the parsley packet with string or a rubber band. Before serving, discard the parsley so your not picking shards of herbs and peppercorns out of your nicely cooked fish.

HERE'S ANOTHER TIP: When you poach fish, keep heat at a simmer or the fish will overcook and fall apart. Always cook fish 10 minutes per inch of thickness.

COOKING PLAN: *Simmer salmon in a flavored broth until done, coat with pesto and serve.*

> 1 pound salmon fillets or steaks
> Salt and pepper
> 2 cups water
> 2 cups bottled clam juice or fish broth
> 1 bouquet garni composed of a bay leaf, 5 whole
>   peppercorns, 1 teaspoon of dried Herbs de

Provence, thyme or oregano and a bunch of
fresh parsley (see tip above)
½ cup pesto, homemade or commercial

Season the salmon lightly with salt and pepper.

Bring the water, clam juice or fish broth and herb bouquet
garni to a boil. Reduce the heat to a medium simmer. Slide
in the salmon and cover.

Cook for 5-8 minutes depending on the thickness of the
salmon, approximately 10 minutes per inch. Turn once
during the cooking period. Remove when it is pink in the
center but before it is falling apart. If it looks ever so
slightly underdone, it will continue cooking in its own heat
while you finish dinner prep.

Remove the salmon to a platter and allow to drain for a few
seconds to remove excess poaching liquid. Coat the salmon
with the pesto and serve immediately.

Serves 4

Sole Muniere, Microwave Style

For eons, French chefs have been cooking thin slivers of sole in butter, lemon and capers for a quick, sophisticated entrée. Use the microwave to steam the fish, which is similar to poaching, but faster.

COOKING PLAN: *Microwave fish on oiled, covered platter. Serve with lemon juice, butter and capers.*

> 1 tablespoon grapeseed or other mild oil
> 4 sole fillets
> Salt and pepper
> Half a lemon
> 2 tablespoons butter
> 2 tablespoons capers

Coat a microwaveable dish large enough to hold the fillets with the oil.

Arrange the fish fillets tightly together on the plate but do not allow them to overlap.

Season lightly with the salt and pepper and squirt the juice from the lemon over the fish.

Place a film of plastic wrap or an inverted plate over the fish. Microwave on full power for 2 minutes. Exact time will depend on the power of your oven. Carefully uncover the fish and test for doneness, that is when it is white but not falling apart.

Return fish to the microwave for a few seconds more if necessary, but don't overcook it. Dot the fish with the butter and scatter the capers on top. Serve immediately.

Serves 4

60

Quick Salmon with Brie Tapenade Sauce

Another take on quick-cooking poached salmon. The rich, tangy sauce is surprisingly easy and will turn an ordinary week night dinner into a culinary event. Remember: always cook fish 10 minutes per inch of thickness. You can substitute your favorite meaty, firm-fleshed fish for the salmon.

COOKING PLAN: *Poach salmon in a skillet with flavored broth, add Brie and olive tapenade and serve.*

> 1 cup water
> 1 cup bottled clam juice or homemade, frozen fish broth
> ½ cup chopped onion
> 1 clove garlic, minced
> Salt and pepper to taste
> Juice of half a lemon
> 4 salmon fillets or steaks
> 8 ounces Brie cheese
> ¼ cup olive tapenade, jarred or homemade, or minced pitted olives

In a covered skillet large enough to hold the salmon in one layer, add the water, onion, garlic, salt, pepper and lemon juice. Bring to a rolling boil and immediately reduce the heat to a simmer.

Add the salmon and cover. Simmer for about 8 minutes or until the salmon is pink in the center but not translucent. Exact time will depend on the thickness of the salmon.

Place the salmon on a serving platter and immediately bring the poaching liquid to a boil. Continue to boil until the liquid has reduced to about a half cup, approximately 5 minutes.

Reduce the heat to a simmer and add the Brie. Stir until it has melted and the sauce is creamy. Stir in the olive tapenade, season for taste with salt and pepper and coat the salmon with the sauce. Serve immediately.

Serves 4

MEAT

A generation of baby boomers grew up on meat, vegetables and potatoes as the standard weeknight menu. In recent history, red meat has become the whipping boy for health-conscious diners. While it is true that a steady diet of gi-normous well-marbled rib eyes flirts with many nasty health problems, from obesity to strokes and heart attacks, meat certainly has a well-deserved place at your table.

The key to health conscious meat eating is portion size, as well as restricting it to two or three times a week. You can stretch your meat rations by blending them with other filling ingredients so that the meal is flavored with beef but not dominated by it.

Get in the habit, if you don't already, to seek out grass-fed beef not contaminated by feed loaded with antibiotics and other chemicals.

Steak Fajitas

Seasoned well and topped with your favorite quick accompaniments, these classic fajitas will have you getting dinner to the table before the crowd knows they are hungry.

HERE'S A TIP: If you are short on your five fruits and veggies for the day, stir in some steamed broccoli or zucchini as well.

COOKING PLAN*: Have ready your favorite toppings—see below. Marinate the steak briefly before cooking. Meanwhile cook vegetables, then steak and serve in tortillas with toppings.*

2 teaspoons of Healthy in a Hurry Fajita Seasoning, homemade (recipe follows) or commercial
1 1/2 tablespoon olive oil
Juice from one lime
1 pound New York strip steak, skirt steak or sirloin, cut against the grain in approximately 1/3rd inch strips
2 tablespoons olive oil
1 medium onion, sliced
1 clove garlic, minced
3 fresh peppers, choosing a mix of red, yellow and green, cut in half, seeds removed and sliced in thin strips
1 Jalapeno pepper, seeded and diced, optional (substitute hot sauce if desired)
Salt and pepper to taste
2 tablespoons lime juice
¼ cup chopped cilantro
8 flour tortillas

Combine the fajita seasoning, olive oil and lime juice in a plastic bag. Add the steak, seal the bag and shake until the beef is coated with the marinade. Refrigerate for at least 20 minutes and several hours if desired.

While the steak is marinating, heat the oil in a large skillet until it is steaming but not burning. Add the onions, garlic, peppers and Jalapeño and stir well. Season with salt and pepper and lime juice.

Cook over medium high heat for 10 minutes or until the vegetables are softened but still slightly crunchy, stirring frequently. Do not allow them to brown.

Wrap tortillas in paper towels and microwave for 5-10 seconds or until heated through. Exact time will depend on the power of your oven. Cover and set aside to keep warm.

Remove the vegetables to a serving platter. Add the steak to the skillet, adding another tablespoon of oil if necessary. Cook over medium high heat until the desired degree of doneness, about 5 minutes. Do not overcook.

Quickly assemble the fajitas by mounding the steak, cilantro and cooked vegetables on one half of a tortilla. Sprinkle with lime juice and add desired toppings. Fold in thirds and serve immediately with your favorite toppings.

Serves 4

Choose one or more of these suggested toppings:

> Marinated Red Onions (see Fish Tacos)
> Fresh or bottled salsa
> Mexican crema or light sour cream thinned slightly
>   with milk

Mix of shredded Monterey Jack and Cheddar
        cheese, about one cup
Chopped tomato
Guacamole or one peeled and diced avocado
2 limes cut in quarters

Healthy in a Hurry Fajita Seasoning

The recipe makes enough for several fajita blowouts. Store what you don't use in a tightly covered container in your cupboard. Stick it in the back away from light to keep the ingredients fresh. If you have a few minutes and a spice grinder handy, toast whole cumin seeds and grind them yourself. It will raise this mix to new heights.

1 tablespoon cornstarch
2 tablespoons ancho or other chili powder
1 tablespoon Maldon or other sea salt
1 tablespoon smoked paprika
1 teaspoon onion powder
1 teaspoon garlic powder
1 teaspoon sugar
1/2 teaspoon ground cumin
1/2 teaspoon cayenne pepper
¼ teaspoon ground cinnamon
Pinch of ground allspice

Place all ingredients in a bowl and blend thoroughly. Store in a covered container in a dark, dry place for a month.

Grilled London Broil with Mustard Glaze

There are no red alerts for tricky ingredients or cooking steps here. Almost an instant dish and oh, so good.

HERE'S A TIP: Line your broiler pan with foil for easy cleaning.

COOKING PLAN: *Blend the first three ingredients. Brush on the meat, broil or grill and serve.*

> ¼ cup whole grain mustard
> ¼ cup soy sauce
> Pepper
> 1 pound London broil

Stir the mustard and soy sauce together until well blended.

Lightly pepper both sides of the beef, then coat with the glaze and set aside for 10 minutes.

Place the beef under the broiler for 5 minutes. Turn and continue to cook for the desired degree of doneness. Serve immediately.

Serves 4

Minute Steak with Sweet Horseradish Cream

The name says it all. Sometimes called cube steak, minute steaks are cut from the top round, then pounded thin until tender. They are ideal for pan sautéing as they cook too quickly for grilling or broiling. You will recognize them by their cross-hatching from the tenderizing hammer. Use the Sweet Horseradish Cream on any beef, from hamburgers to prime rib.

HERE'S A TIP: Don't turn your back on the meat. It cooks in a flash and you don't want to render it tough by overcooking.

HERE'S ANOTHER TIP: To prevent meat and chicken from sticking to the pan when frying or sautéing, be sure the oil is hot enough. It should pop and sizzle in the pan but not scorch. If the meat sticks, the pan was too cool.

COOKING PLAN: Assemble the Sweet Horseradish Cream and set aside. Sauté the steaks and serve.

3 tablespoons olive oil
1 clove garlic, minced
Salt and pepper to taste
4 minute or cube steaks
Cooking spray or olive oil

Combine olive oil, garlic, salt and pepper in small bowl and brush evenly on both sides of the meat. Cover and refrigerate from 15 minutes to several hours.

Coat a heavy bottomed skillet pan with cooking spray and heat until a spray of water sizzles. Important to have the pan very hot or the meat will stick to the pan.

Place the meat on the pan and add salt to the top of the meat. Cook for one minute, turn, salt the top and cook for 1 more minute.

Serve immediately with the Sweet Horseradish Cream.

Serves 4

Sweet Horseradish Cream

¼ cup light sour cream
½ teaspoon horseradish or to taste
½ teaspoon sugar or to taste

Blend all ingredients until smooth, taste and season again if desired. Place in a covered container until cooking time.

Beef and Bleu Cheese Quesadillas

Using top quality deli beef or leftover steak makes quick work of delicious one-dish favorite.

COOKING PLAN: *Assemble ingredients, fill tortillas and pan fry.*

1 tablespoon olive oil
¼ cup red onion, thinly sliced
½ red pepper, thinly sliced
3 tablespoons sweet mustard
3 tablespoons light sour cream
4 whole wheat tortillas
½ pound thinly sliced deli beef
2 tablespoons crumbled Bleu, feta or goat cheese
Cooking spray or 1 tablespoon olive oil

Heat the olive oil until just steaming in a heavy skillet. Do not let the oil brown or burn. Add onion and peppers and stir for 2 minutes or until they are soft but not brown.

Combine the mustard and sour cream, blend until smooth and spread on the whole wheat tortillas. Fill the tortillas with the onions, peppers, beef and cheese.

Fold each in half. Wipe out the skillet with a paper towel and coat lightly with cooking spray or olive oil. Heat until steaming and add 2 quesadillas. Cook 2 minutes on each side or until lightly browned.

Set aside on a serving platter and cover with foil to keep warm. Add more cooking spray to pan and cook remaining 2 quesadillas and serve immediately while hot.

Serves 4

Pork Chops with Dried Fruit Sauce and Oven-Roasted Yams

Here is a sweet alternative to the classic pairing of pork and applesauce made easy with a microwaved dried fruit sauce. The perfect accompaniment is yams, which you just stick in the oven to roast. Roasting yams—not sweet potatoes--naked in a hot oven caramelizes the sweet flesh in half the time it takes to bake a potato. While you can give it a lick of butter if you wish, it needs no adornment for a luscious and very low cal and filling side dish.

My favorite tenderizing trick for pork, chicken breasts and even fish is to marinate it in a dairy product. The lactic acid in milk, buttermilk and yogurt produces a lovely, tender texture.

Also, butterflying the chops as described (if you haven't done this before, it only takes a second or two with a sharp knife) discourages overcooking that can toughen the meat.

COOKING PLAN: Stick yams in the oven to roast. Microwave the apple mixture. Butterfly the chops (unless your butcher will do it for you). Marinate the pork in milk briefly. Dry and coat with seasonings. Pan fry and serve with the apples and yams.

Preheat oven to 400 degrees F.

Medium size garnet or jewel yams, one per person

1 cup mixed dried fruit, either whole fruit or
    chopped
1/4 cup raisins or dried cranberries
¼ cup apple juice

¼ cup water
1 tablespoon sugar
Large pinch of cinnamon
Large pinch of pumpkin pie spices
1 tablespoon lemon juice

4 boneless pork chops, about one inch thick
1 cup milk, buttermilk or plain yogurt
2 tablespoons lemon pepper or other preferred herb
    seasoning for meat
2 tablespoons extra virgin olive oil
1 tablespoon butter
Generous pinch of ground cinnamon

Place the yams whole and unpeeled on a baking sheet covered with foil and roast until tender about half an hour. Slip off the skins and serve. May be made ahead and reheated in the microwave.

Place the dried fruit, raisins, apple juice, water, sugar, cinnamon, spices and lemon juice in a flat microwaveable baking dish and stir. Fruit should be just covered with liquid so add more water if necessary. Cook uncovered on high until the fruit has softened and the juices are syrupy, about 2-3 minutes. Exact time will depend on your oven. Set aside. May be made ahead and stored covered in the refrigerator for several days and reheated at serving time.

Meanwhile, butterfly the pork chops by imagining they are books you are about to open. Slice into them with a very sharp knife from one edge to just ½ inch from the other edge. Do not cut them into two pieces. Open them up and gently flatten down the center. You will have a large, thin cut of meat.

Place the pork in a baking dish and cover with milk. Allow to sit for at least 10 minutes and up to 1 hour while the apples and yams are cooking.

Ten minutes before serving, remove the pork and discard the milk. Dry thoroughly (don't rinse) and coat with the lemon pepper.

Heat the remaining oil and butter in a skillet large enough to hold the pork in one layer (cook in two pans if necessary or two batches). Stir in the cinnamon and when just sizzling, add the pork.

Cook over medium high heat for 4 minutes on each side or until the pork is white in the center with perhaps a slight pink tinge. Do not overcook.

Serve immediately with the fruit sauce and yams.

Serves 4

POULTRY

You'll never run out of ways to tuck lean poultry into a dinner menu, whether it is fresh, leftover or roasted to a golden hue on your local market's rotisserie. Lean cuts, such as breast meat or boneless thighs and drumsticks, offer many options for last minute meals. They provide the perfect canvas for the menu helpers in your pantry, such as chutney and glazes, as they need very little cooking and flavoring to produce enticing meals. Just be sure you buy free range for the healthiest poultry options.

Turkey Apricot Sliders

Yes, you can make these sliders with chicken, but think turkey for a very tasty dinner entrée. Turkey cutlets have the extra added attraction of being very VERY lean, a boon to the calorie conscious. By the way, you want the chunky preserves in this sauce, not jam or jelly. And yes, the poultry seasoning is the one you use once a year for dressing the Thanksgiving turkey. That familiar sage flavor enriches these sliders.

HERE'S A TIP: This barbecue sauce is crazy simple. Keep leftover on hand to use on grilled chicken and pork.

COOKING PLAN: Assemble the ingredients for the Apricot Barbecue Sauce and set aside. Season the turkey and pan fry, then stack on the buns. Brush with the sauce and serve.

    1/2 teaspoon freshly ground black pepper
    1/8 teaspoon salt
    Pinch of poultry seasoning
    2 tablespoons extra virgin olive oil
    1 1/2 pounds skinless, boneless turkey cutlets
    Apricot Barbecue Sauce (recipe follows)
    Mayonnaise
    Baby spinach leaves
    Red onion slices
    8 mini burger buns

Combine the salt, pepper, poultry seasoning and 1 tablespoon of the oil in a small bowl and brush on both sides of the turkey cutlets.

Add the remaining oil to a heavy bottomed skillet and heat until smoking but not burning. Add the turkey.

Cook on each side for 2-3 minutes or until done but not overcooked. Meat should be white in the center, not pink.

Allow to cool briefly until you can handle the meat, paint lightly with the Apricot Barbecue Sauce, then tear it into large shreds. Turkey can be done ahead at this point.

Lightly coat the buns with mayonnaise and heat briefly under the broiler. Mound the turkey, spinach and onion on the bottom of the rolls, drizzle liberally with the Apricot Barbecue Sauce, add the top half of the bun and serve immediately.

Serves 4

Apricot Barbecue Sauce

3 tablespoons apricot preserves
1 tablespoon water
1 teaspoon cider vinegar
1 tablespoon Dijon mustard or other favorite
    mustard, but NOT yellow (try sweet and beer
    mustards as well)

Place all the ingredients in a microwaveable bowl and heat gently until just bubbly and steaming. Do not overcook. Exact time will depend on the power of your oven. Stir thoroughly and store covered in the refrigerator if not using immediately. Will last for several days.

Turkey Cutlets with Mustard Cream

This is a grownup take on easy turkey cutlets. The mustard cream is a no-fuss shortcut to a wine sauce that is a great option for a quick meal.

COOKING PLAN: *Pan fry the turkey, cook down the juices and make a simple wine sauce that is finished with cream and mustard.*

> Salt and pepper
> 1 pound turkey cutlets
> 1 tablespoon olive oil
> 1 tablespoon butter
> ½ cup chicken broth, or ¼ cup chicken broth and ¼ cup dry Vermouth or other dry white wine
> 2 tablespoons Dijon mustard
> 3 tablespoons heavy cream or half and half
> Lightly salt and pepper both sides of the cutlets

Heat the oil and butter in a heavy bottomed skillet, large enough to hold the turkey in one layer. If necessary, use two small skillets but do not overcrowd the pan. When drops of water dissolve (if the pan does not get hot enough, the turkey will stick to the pan), add the cutlets.

Cook for three minutes on each side over medium-high heat or until the turkey is white in the center. Do not overcook.

Remove the turkey to a platter and cover with foil to keep warm.

To the juices in the pan, add the chicken broth and wine if you are using it. Raise the heat to high and stirring constantly, scrape up the juices and browned bits for about

5 minutes or until the liquid has cooked down to approximately half.

Stir in the mustard and cream and blend thoroughly. If there are juices in the platter, add them to the pan. Taste for seasoning and add salt and pepper if necessary. Pour the sauce over the turkey and serve immediately.

Serves 4

Chicken Quesadillas

My family could not have survived without these fabulous, instant Mexican grilled cheese sandwiches.

COOKING PLAN: *Assemble the filling for the quesadillas. Fill and fold the tortillas and pan fry. Serve with desired toppings.*

2 cooked chicken breasts, coarsely shredded
1 cup Monterey Jack Cheese
1 whole egg
1-2 tablespoons diced, canned chilies, or one fresh
    Jalapeno, seeded and chopped for more fire
4 flour tortillas
1 tablespoon extra virgin olive oil
1 tablespoon butter

Choose one or more of these suggested toppings:

Marinated Red Onions (see Fish Tacos)
½ avocado, peeled and diced or ½ cup guacamole
¼ cup light sour cream
½ cup fresh or bottled salsa

In a medium size mixing bowl combine the chicken, cheese, egg and chili. Blend thoroughly.

Spoon the mixture onto the tortillas and fold each in half.

Heat the oil and butter until it just sizzles and add the quesadillas. Cook over medium high heat until golden on the underside, about 1-2 minutes. Turn and cook until the other side is browned as well. Serve immediately with favorite toppings.

Serves 4

Grilled Chicken with Hoisin Dipping Sauce

This quick gingery chicken is a good contrast to the sweet Hoisin Dipping Sauce. Reserve a little of the marinade to paint on the chicken at the end of the cooking time. You never want to contaminate cooked chicken with the juice or marinade from raw chicken.

HERE'S A TIP: When you have a grilling sauce containing sugar, always paint it on the food during the last 5 minutes of cooking or the sugar will burn and scorch the food.

COOKING PLAN: Prepare Hoisin Dipping Sauce, fire up the grill, marinate the chicken briefly, grill and serve.

> 1 pound boned chicken breasts, all skin and fat removed
> Juice of 1 orange
> 1 green onion, minced
> 1 teaspoon or move minced fresh ginger
> Hoisin Dipping Sauce (recipe follows)

Prepare the grill. Place the chicken breasts in a shallow dish. In a small bowl, blend the orange juice, onion and ginger and reserve 2-3 tablespoons of the marinade in a separate bowl. Pour the remainder over the chicken. Cover and refrigerate for at least 20 minutes and turn the chicken once or twice as it marinates.

Grill the chicken 3 to 4 minutes on each side, depending on the thickness. Turn the breasts frequently and during the last minute, paint with the reserved marinade and some of the Hoisin Dipping Sauce.

Continue cooking until the chicken is firm to the touch, the meat is white at the center and the juices run clear. Do not overcook. Serve immediately with the remaining Hoisin Dipping Sauce.

Serves 4

Hoisin Dipping Sauce

Hoisin is a Chinese fermented mixture with a consistency between a sauce and a paste. It has soy as its base, but that description gives no hint of the complex and delicious flavors that meld into a dark purée, which resonates with hot pepper, ginger, sesame and sugar. The overall sensation is sweet, which perhaps is why the flavor is so seductive. Different brands emphasize salt over sugar or garlic rather than ginger. Try several to find the one you prefer. You can find the bottled sauce in Chinese markets or in the international foods section of supermarkets and specialty websites. You can also add a drop or two of Asian sesame oil.

> 1/2 cup hoisin sauce
> 3 to 4 tablespoons fresh orange juice, more if
>   desired

Blend all the ingredients in a small serving bowl and taste. Add more orange juice if you wish. Pass with the chicken.

Chicken Breasts with Pear and Bleu Cheese

In this no-fuss main dish, chicken breasts, sweet pear and tangy Bleu cheese are a match made in heaven. This easy duo of stovetop and oven cooking produces unbelievably tender chicken. Covering the chicken in both foil and the lid before you put it in the oven is a semi-braising method that you can use for chicken, turkey cutlets and fish. Be sure the oil is very hot before you add the chicken so it does not stick to the pan.

HERE'S A TIP: If you haven't used grapeseed oil, give it a try. You may find that it is a bit pricey, but if a bottle doesn't break your budget, it is an excellent cooking oil, with a mild flavor and high smoking point. In addition, it is one of the best heart-healthy oils you can use.

COOKING PLAN: Quickly prepare the pears. Pan-fry the chicken, top with pears and cheese, finish cooking in the oven and serve.

Preheat oven to 375 degrees F

> 1 small ripe Bartlett pear
> 1 tablespoon grapeseed or other mild oil
> 1 pound boneless, skinless chicken breasts
> Salt and pepper
> ¼ cup crumbled Bleu cheese

Slice the pear in quarters and carve out the core. Slice each quarter in ½ inch thick slices and set aside.

In a heavy skillet large enough to hold the chicken in one layer, heat the oil but do not allow it to burn. Lightly season the chicken with salt and pepper and add to the skillet.

Cook the chicken on each side for 1 minute or until lightly browned.

Arrange the pear slices over the chicken (munch on any left over slices) and cover with foil, pressing it tightly over the chicken. Cover with a lid and place in the preheated oven for 10 minutes or until the chicken is springy to the touch and the juices run clear, not red or pink.

Arrange the chicken and pears on a serving dish and sprinkle with the Bleu cheese, which will melt into the hot pears. Serve immediately.

Serves 4

Easy Chicken Parmesan

On date night I like to dredge the chicken in an egg batter and homemade breadcrumbs to get that distinctive crust. Heck, I'll even make my own tomato sauce. But after a day of keeping body, soul, job and family together, I opt for this quick, one pan version of an old favorite. As with most tomato sauced dishes, leftovers are even better the second day. Don't forget to pound the chicken so it isn't too thick or it won't cook thoroughly. I love this step as a stress-reliever. Get into it!

COOKING PLAN: *Arrange chicken in a baking pan, layer with sauce, breadcrumbs, cheese and bake.*

Preheat oven to 375 degrees F.

> Salt and pepper
> 2 tablespoons olive oil
> 4 boneless, skinless chicken breasts
> 4 slices mozzarella cheese, 2 inches wide, ½ inch thick
> 2 cups marinara or favorite commercial or homemade tomato sauce
> 2 cups herb-flavored breadcrumbs
> 1 cup shredded mozzarella cheese, more if desired
> ½ cup grated Parmesan cheese, more if desired

If your chicken breasts are very thick, place them between plastic wrap on a flat surface and pound several times with a heavy pot or skillet to flatten it to no more than two inches thick. Since it is not going to be browned first, this will ensure that it cooks through. Salt and pepper the chicken.

Add the oil to an ovenproof baking dish or skillet large enough to hold the chicken in one layer. Arrange the chicken evenly on the bottom.

Pour half the marinara sauce over the chicken. Sprinkle half the mozzarella and Parmesan cheeses evenly over the sauce. Add the remaining sauce, and the breadcrumbs, then the remaining cheeses.

Bake in the preheated oven for 35 minutes or until the chicken is firm and the juices run clear. Serve immediately.

Serves 4

PASTA AND PIZZA

Crowd favorites always, these two entrees are ideal canvases for putting together easy meals. Make a quick, nourishing pasta with favorite vegetables and cheeses or top store-bought pizza crusts with commercial tomato sauce and your favorite deli meats, cheeses and greens. Your gang won't be able to get to the dining table fast enough.

Spaghetti Pesto with Potatoes, Beans and Olives

Potatoes and pasta? Isn't that overkill? Not if you are in Naples, where this is a favored match. Choose this for an easy, filling main dish.

HERE'S A TIP: In this yummy version, choose sweet, new potatoes that will hold their texture and not melt into the pasta as a baking potato would.

COOKING PLAN*: Cook potatoes and bacon, stir into the remaining ingredients, toss with pesto, cheese, fresh basil and season to taste before serving.*

>12 ounces spaghetti
>10 baby spring potatoes, cut in half and steamed
>   until tender (can be prepared ahead, chilled or
>   use left over potatoes)
>1 teaspoon extra virgin olive oil
>2 slices cooked, Applewood or other artisan bacon,
>   diced, or pancetta
>4 ounces thin green beans, ends trimmed and
>   steamed until barely tender
>¼ cup pesto, commercial or homemade
>1 dozen pitted green or black olives
>Grated Parmesan cheese to taste
>4 tablespoons chopped, fresh basil
>Salt and pepper to taste

Cook the spaghetti in a large pot of lightly salted boiling water until just tender, not mushy but cooked through.

Reserve ½ cup of the water in a small cup, drain the spaghetti and return to the pot. Stir in the olive oil until the pasta is well coated.

Add the cooked potatoes, bacon, beans, pesto and olives and blend well. If necessary, stir a few tablespoons of the reserved pasta water for a smooth consistency

Season to taste with salt and pepper. Serve in individual dishes and sprinkle with Parmesan cheese to taste and dot with the basil leaves. Serve immediately.

Serves 4

Rosamarina with Lemon and Herbs

Rosamarina is a rice-shaped pasta often used in soups. Happily, it cooks much faster than rice. I like it here dressed up as a quick accompaniment to fish or chicken. If you can't find rosamarina, orzo will work as well but you may need to boil it a minute or so longer. Also a member of the pasta family, orzo is a slightly larger shape.

COOKING PLAN: *This couldn't be easier. Cook the pasta, drain and stir in the remaining ingredients.*

½ pound rosamarina
1 lemon
1 tablespoon olive oil
1 tablespoon fresh marjoram
½ cup Italian parsley, minced
Salt and freshly ground pepper
Parmesan cheese to taste

Add the rosamarina to a pot of lightly salted boiling water. Cook for 7 minutes or until tender. Drain thoroughly and set aside.

Meanwhile, peel a 2-inch strip from the lemon peel (just the colored part not the white pith). Mince it finely and blend with the marjoram and parsley. Set aside.

Heat the oil in a skillet and add the lemon and herb mixture. Stir for about one minute or until the green of the herbs intensifies. Season with salt and pepper, add the rosamarina and stir thoroughly. Taste for seasoning, adding a squirt of lemon juice if desired. Add the Parmesan cheese and serve immediately.

Serves 4

Pasta Omelet with Fresh Tomatoes and Basil

Try this unusual but wildly tasty hybrid of a dish for a Sunday night supper. Read the Cooking Plan before you start if you think this sounds like too much trouble. This is a dish I introduced to my cooking students years ago. Every time I presented it, people were agape at how quickly it came together.

COOKING PLAN: Cook the pasta and set aside. Sauté tomatoes and mix with pasta. Make the omelet and fill with pasta and tomatoes, season with salt, pepper, basil and cheese and serve.

> 1 ½ ounces fusilli or other short pasta
> 1 tablespoon extra virgin olive oil
> 1 tablespoon butter
> 1 small garlic clove, minced
> 2 medium tomatoes, seeded and chopped
> 2-3 tablespoons finely chopped fresh basil leaves
> Salt and pepper to taste
> 4 eggs, beaten and reserved in a bowl
> 1 tablespoon finely chopped fresh basil
> ¼ cup freshly grated Parmesan cheese

In a pot of boiling, salted water, cook the pasta until tender, but not mush, about 5-7 minutes. Drain and set aside.

Heat the oil and butter in a medium size skillet until the butter has melted but not browned. Add the garlic and stir over medium heat for a minute or so until softened but not browned.

Add the tomatoes and basil to the garlic, turn the heat high and stir over the heat until softened and very hot, 2 minutes or so. Do not overcook or the tomatoes will release too much liquid.

Stir in the pasta and half the cheese, season with salt and pepper and set aside.

Brush a medium-size skillet or seasoned omelet pan with cooking spray or butter and heat until just smoking but not burning. Pour the eggs into the pan and allow to spread over the surface. The bottom will cook quickly and the top will be runny and then custardy as they begin to set. Season with salt and pepper.

As it cooks, gently loosen the underside of the omelet with a spatula and rotate the pan to allow the uncooked egg to hit the hot surface of the skillet.

When just about cooked, add the pasta and tomato mixture and fold over half the omelet. Cook for another half minute or so until the center is set. Shake it onto a serving plate and serve with a sprinkling of cheese.

Serves 4

Pita Pizza

Have your crowd prepare their own pizzas. Set up an assembly station with pitas, sauce, deli meats, cheeses—whatever strikes your fancy. Then stick them under the broiler for a minute or two. Without a crust to bake, the cooking time is very short. Here are some suggestions for toppings, but you can use your favorites. Just don't use raw vegetables like peppers or meats that need a longer time in the oven or the pita will burn.

COOKING PLAN: *Stack the pitas with your choice of toppings and broil quickly*

Cooking spray
4 whole wheat pitas
½ cup pizza sauce
1 jar red peppers
½ pound goat cheese
6 sun dried tomatoes in oil, coarsely chopped
Fresh basil leaves

Coat a cookie sheet with a light film of cooking spray. Place the pitas on the cookie sheet and brush with the pizza sauce. Divide the red peppers, goat cheese and sun dried tomatoes evenly among the pitas and place in the oven for 7-10 minutes or until peppers are hot and the goat cheese has softened.

Remove from the oven and sprinkle with the fresh basil. Serve immediately.

Serves 4

Pizza with Prosciutto, Arugula and Gorgonzola

This pizza was inspired by a dinner at Mozza's in Los Angeles, known for their exquisite, authentic Italian menu, but especially their pizzas. You can't duplicate their thin, delectable crusts in half an hour, so I have improvised here with a commercial crust and some easy toppings.

COOKING PLAN: *Mound ingredients on crust and cook until done.*

Preheat oven to 425 degrees F.

> 1 Boboli or other commercial pizza crust
> 1 tablespoon extra virgin olive oil
> 8 slices prosciutto
> 2 cups arugula, washed and dried
> ½ cup Gorgonzola or other veined cheese, crumbled
> ¼ cup Parmesan cheese

Brush the pizza crust with the olive oil and arrange the prosciutto, arugula and Gorgonzola on the crust. Sprinkle with Parmesan cheese and bake in the oven for 5 minutes or until the cheese has melted. Serve immediately.

Serves 4

SALADS

Forget salads as an appit-easer, those standard greens with a splash of dressing out of a bottle served before or after the main event because—well, aren't you supposed to? I'm talking main course salads muscled up with chicken or fish, beans or grains, vegetables, fruits, nuts . . . heck you can empty the whole refrigerator into a bowl and with a perfectly balanced dressing (homemade!!!!) have a gut-filling wonder meal in under 15 minutes. Here are a few suggestions.

Smoked Salmon and Artichoke Salad

Here is where your well-stocked pantry will come in handy. Everything for this Mediterranean inspired meal-in-a-salad is out of a jar, ones that you bought in a specialty shop so you know they are delicious and healthful. If you can find Silver Lining Smoked Salmon, snap it up, though there are other admirable brands easily available.

COOKING PLAN: There isn't one—just get out your can or jar opener and spoon everything into your favorite, decorative bowl, whisk the dressing together, toss and serve.

    1 can smoked salmon
    ½ cup sun-dried tomatoes, chopped
    1 roasted red bell pepper, cut in strips, freshly
        roasted or bottled
    ½ cup pitted green or black olives
    2 tablespoons capers
    ¼ cup minced Italian parsley
    4 cups mixed greens
    Herb Mustard Dressing (recipe follows)

Into a large bowl add the salmon, breaking it into flakes, sun-dried tomatoes, pepper, olives capers and parsley. Add enough of the dressing to thoroughly moisten everything without leaving it soggy.

Serves 4

Herb Mustard Dressing

½ cup extra virgin olive oil
3 tablespoons balsamic vinegar
1 heaping tablespoon Dijon or other favorite French
    mustard
1 teaspoon dried Herbs de Provence, or fresh thyme
    or oregano
Salt and pepper to taste

In a small mixing bowl, add all the ingredients and whisk
until smooth. Taste and adjust seasoning if necessary.
Store any remaining dressing in a tightly covered
container in the refrigerator for up to ten days.

Yam and Black Bean Salad

Looking for a way to squeeze in your five daily veggies? This meal-in-a-salad bowl offers up an easy and delicious solution. Forego a bottled dressing for the easy and original Spicy Orange Dressing. You can also add cut up cooked chicken breast to add protein and bulk to the salad.

HERE'S A TIP: When you are on the run, instead of peeling and cubing the yams—easier actually than peeling white potatoes--speed up the prep work by slicing the yams, seasoning them and roasting them unpeeled. When they are cooked, it is much easier to simply slide off the skins around the sides and cut the slices in 1-inch cubes.

COOKING PLAN: Don't let the list of ingredients scare you off. There is very little cooking here. While the yams are roasting, make the dressing and set aside and assemble the remaining salad ingredients in a bowl. Finish up with the yams, toss with the dressing, mound on the greens and dinner is done and done!

Preheat the oven to 425 degrees F.

> 4 medium yams, preferably Garnets or Jewels, peeled and cut into approximately 1-inch cubes but no larger
> 3 tablespoons extra virgin olive oil
> 1/2 tablespoon ground coriander
> 1/2 tablespoon chili powder
> 1/2 tablespoon ground cumin
> 1 teaspoon fine sea salt
> 2 cups corn niblets, fresh or frozen and thawed (if they are very sweet I do not cook them,

otherwise microwave for a few seconds before
using)
1/2 cup fresh red pepper, seeded and diced
2 15½ ounce cans black beans, drained and rinsed
¼ cup thinly sliced scallions
1/2 cup chopped cilantro
4 cups mixed greens
Spicy Orange Dressing (recipe follows)

In a mixing bowl, blend the oil, coriander, chili powder, cumin, and salt. Toss well with the yams until they are evenly coated.

Spray a baking sheet with a light film of cooking spray and spread the yams evenly in one layer. Bake for approximately 15-20 minutes or until tender but not mushy.

Meanwhile, add the remaining ingredients except the salad greens to a large salad bowl and toss well with 2-3 tablespoons of the dressing.

When the yams are cooked, add to the salad and toss gently with enough of the Spicy Orange dressing to moisten the salad thoroughly but not enough to make it soggy.

Mound the greens on serving place, add the salad and serve.

Serves 4

Spicy Orange Dressing

Also delicious on chicken and fruit salads. This makes enough for several salads. Store any remainder covered in the refrigerator for up to 2 weeks.

> ¼ cup freshly squeezed orange juice
> ¼ teaspoon grated orange zest
> Juice of half a lime
> 2 tablespoons white balsamic, raspberry or red wine vinegar
> 2 teaspoons minced shallot
> 1 teaspoon sweet mustard
> Hot sauce to taste
> 6 tablespoons extra virgin olive oil
> Salt and pepper to taste

Whisk all ingredients together in a small bowl until smooth. Taste and adjust seasonings, adding more hot sauce, salt or pepper as desired

Warm Mexican Chicken Salad Wrap

Aficionados of Mexican cuisine will recognize the tostada influence here, the chicken salad served in a deep fried tortilla. This knockoff heats everything in the oven on a healthful whole-wheat tortilla for a quick one-stop salad in a wrap.

HERE'S A TIP: Use cooked rotisserie chicken from your local market and buy shredded cheese.

COOKING PLAN: Mound chicken, cheese and beans on the tortillas and bake. Top with remaining ingredients, wrap as for a burrito and serve.

Preheat oven to 450 degrees F.

> Cooking spray
> 4 whole wheat tortillas
> ½ cup cooked chicken, diced
> 1 cup black or refried beans
> 1 cup shredded Cheddar or Monterey Jack cheese, or a mixture
> 1 cup shredded iceberg lettuce
> 1¼ cup sliced black or green olives
> 1 Jalapeno pepper, halved, seeds removed and diced (or to taste)
> 1 cup favorite fresh or bottled salsa
> Commercial or homemade guacamole
> 1/3 cup light sour cream
> ¼ cup coarsely chopped fresh cilantro

Coat a cookie sheet with a light film of cooking spray. Place the tortillas on the cookie sheet and mound each one with equal portions of chicken, beans and cheese. Place in the oven for 10 minutes or until the chicken and beans are hot and the cheese has melted.

Top each tortilla with the shredded lettuce, olives, Jalapeno, salsa, guacamole and sour cream. Sprinkle with the cilantro, wrap and serve immediately.

Serves 4

Potato, Green Bean and Caper Salad with Pesto

Add cold chicken, salmon or tuna to this zesty salad for a one-dish meal. Or, serve with a rotisserie chicken from the market.

COOKING PLAN: The only cooking here is a light steaming of the potato or beans. Dress them with capers and a jar of pesto and there you have it.

1 pound baby red potatoes, halved
1 pound fresh green beans, ends trimmed
3 tablespoons capers, drained (if you use salted—
    the best in my opinion—rinsed in cold water)
Salt and pepper
1/2 cup basil pesto, homemade or commercial

In a steamer, cook the potatoes for 15 minutes or until tender. Turn into a mixing bowl and allow to cool slightly.

Add the beans to the steamer and cook for 3-4 minutes until still bright green and crunchy.

Toss the potatoes and beans with the capers, season with salt and pepper—note that the capers will add salt, so tread carefully.

Stir in half the pesto and toss until everything is coated, adding more pesto if necessary. Serve while still warm.

Serves 4

Carrot and Broccoli Salad with Orange Honey Dressing

This healthful salad has the most potent and delicious disease-fighters in your supermarket. No one wants to approach assembling a menu like designing a medical regimen, but you just can't help feeling good about serving a rich mix of yellow and green veggies in a snappy, oil-free dressing. You can add/substitute cauliflower, squash, mushrooms or beans, if you like.

HERE'S A TIP: Add the dressing to the carrots and broccoli while they are still warm to help the dressing penetrate the vegetables. The key to this salad is to have the vegetables just lightly steamed. Mushy vegetables are never appealing, but particularly disappoint a palate expecting the crunch of a salad.

COOKING PLAN: Steam the vegetables, mix the dressing, toss and serve.

> 1 pound carrots
> 1 pound broccoli florets
> 1 large red pepper, trimmed, seeded and cut in 1-inch squares
> 1/2 sweet, red onion, thinly sliced
> Salt and pepper to taste
> Orange Honey Dressing (recipe follows)

Peel and trim the carrots, cut in thick, lengthwise slices and steam 4-7 minutes until tender but still crisp.

Trim the broccoli into individual florets and steam 4-6 minutes until barely tender.

While hot, place the carrots and broccoli in a serving bowl. Add the red pepper and onion and toss well, seasoning very lightly with the salt and pepper.

Pour the Orange Dressing over the vegetables, tossing thoroughly. Serve at room temperature or chilled.

Serves 4

Orange Honey Dressing

This dressing is terrific on warm beets and winter squashes as well, so keep it in your recipe file.

2 tablespoons red raspberry vinegar
2 tablespoons honey
2 tablespoons Dijon mustard
6 tablespoons fresh orange juice
2 teaspoons fresh lemon juice

Whisk all ingredients together until smooth and toss with warm vegetables.

DESSERTS

Sure, you can keep the brood happy when they scream for dessert by doling out store-bought cookies. But why not pass up the usual commercial stuff touted on TV and surprise them with sweet treats that will have their eyes popping with delight? Here are a few ideas that will fit into your busy schedule and score big with the family.

Roast Pears Helene

Here is a school night version of a classic French dessert. This easy roasting method gives the pears a custardy texture that is delicious even without the toppings.

HERE'S A TIP: To achieve the creamy texture of the pears, do not pierce the skin before you roast them.

COOKING PLAN: Stick the pears in the oven before you start dinner and they will be ready for their simple toppings by the time you are clearing the table.

> 4 ripe Bartlett pears
> 4 shortbread cookies, crumbled
> Hot fudge sauce, commercial or homemade
> Vanilla-flavored Greek yogurt

Preheat oven to 375 degrees F.

Wash the pears but do not bruise, cut the skin or remove the stem. Place a sheet of aluminum foil on the baking sheet and place the pears on the foil. Crumple the foil around the bottom of the pears if necessary to allow them to stand upright. Bake for 30 minutes.

Heat the fudge sauce in the microwave just before serving. Exact time will depend on the power of your oven.

Place each pear on an individual serving dish and spoon the vanilla yogurt and hot fudge sauce over the pears. Sprinkle with the cookie crumbs and serve immediately.

Serves 4

Berry and Melon Soup

Colorful, refreshing and easy. What a delectable way to get your important fresh fruits.

COOKING PLAN: *Place all ingredients in blender, puree, chill until serving time and garnish with mint.*

    12 ounces red raspberries
    1 cup honeydew melon cubes
    1/2 cup fresh orange juice
    1 1/2 cup vanilla-flavored nonfat yogurt
    1 tablespoon sugar or to taste (if your fruit is very
        sweet you may not need it)
    1 tablespoon minced fresh mint

In a blender or food processor, puree the raspberries, melon, juice and yogurt until smooth.

Add the sugar a pinch at a time, blend thoroughly and taste, adding more sugar if necessary. Stop when the soup is refreshingly sweet but not cloying. Chill thoroughly before serving with a sprinkle of mint.

Serves 4

Hot Hot-Banana Splits

Seriously? You mean don't have to live near an old-fashioned soda fountain to indulge in a retro banana split? Read on. These aren't quite what you'd find in Ye Olde Soda Shoppe. But this take on New Orleans' famed Bananas Foster won't have anybody complaining. The indulgence here is hot fudge sauce, tempered by yogurt instead of whipped cream or ice cream.

COOKING PLAN*: Melt the butter with the seasonings, brown the bananas in the butter and spoon over frozen yogurt, top with fudge sauce.*

2 tablespoons butter
2 tablespoons brown sugar
¼ teaspoon ground cinnamon
½ cup fresh orange juice
3 ripe but not browned bananas, peeled and halved
Vanilla frozen yogurt
Hot fudge sauce, commercial or homemade

In a heavy bottomed skillet, melt the butter with the sugar, cinnamon and orange juice, stirring constantly. Add the bananas and stir over high heat until the bananas are golden and tender but not mushy, about 2 minutes. Turn once to brown evenly.

While the bananas cook, heat the fudge sauce in the microwave until melted. Time will depend on the power of your oven, but approximately 8 –10 seconds.

Spoon the bananas and sauce onto serving plates and top with the frozen yogurt. Drizzle with the fudge sauce and serve immediately.

Serves 4

Cherry Pistachio Crisps

You don't have to wait for summer to serve this simple but mouthwatering dessert. If you prefer sour cherries, by all means use them and add an extra tablespoon of sugar with the cornstarch.

HERE'S A TIP: Double the topping recipe and put half in a plastic bag in the freezer to have ready for next time. Use this topping on any cooked fruit desserts.

COOKING PLAN*: Blend the cherry filling ingredients. Blend topping mix, spoon into muffin cups, bake and serve.*

Preheat oven to 350 degrees F.

> 1 8-ounce can of organic pitted Bing or dark, sweet cherries, reserve ¼ cup of juice, then drain but do not rinse cherries
> 1 tablespoon granulated sugar (more if you use sour cherries)
> 1 tablespoon cornstarch
> Pinch of ground cinnamon
> Pinch of salt
> ¼ cup all-purpose flour
> ¼ cup old-fashioned rolled oats (not instant)
> 3 tablespoons firmly packed light brown sugar
> ½ teaspoon ground cinnamon
> Generous pinch of salt
> 4 tablespoons softened butter
> 2 tablespoons chopped pistachios

Spray a 6-cup muffin pan with cooking spray, being sure to coat the top where the crisps might spill over. Fill two cups with water so they do not scorch during baking.

Drain the cherries and place in a bowl with the sugar, cornstarch, lemon juice, cinnamon and salt. Blend well and fill each of the paper-lined molds with the mixture.

In a small food processor or by hand in a bowl blend the remaining ingredients. Do not worry if the butter is a little bit clumpy. Spoon the mixture evenly over the cherries and place in the oven for 20-25 minutes or until the topping is browned. Do not let it scorch. Remove from the oven and let stand at least 5 minutes before serving with a dollop of frozen yogurt or ice cream if desired.

Serves 4

Fig and Raspberry Parfait

I consider this one of the most elegant desserts in my repertoire, which includes many labor-intensive cakes, French pastries and soufflés. That it is quite an endorsement for a sweet treat that you can prepare in an instant. It is the contrast of sweet fig, lush Mascarpone cheese, the delicate Italian cream cheese, and tart raspberries that make this a standout.

COOKING PLAN: *Slice the figs, fill with Mascarpone cheese and raspberries, microwave and serve.*

8 fresh figs
½ cup mascarpone cheese
1 pint fresh raspberries, washed
1 tablespoon sugar

Trim away the stems of the figs and make two crosswise slits but do not cut all the way through. Gently pull open the figs and place in a microwaveable baking dish.

Spoon the Mascarpone cheese into the center of the figs. Then add the raspberries, dust with the sugar and microwave on high for 10-20 seconds until the figs are hot and the cheese has softened. Exact time will depend on the power of your oven. Serve immediately.

Serves 4

Strawberries with Brown Sugar and Sour Cream

If you were invited to a dinner party (remember those?) in the 1970's, chances were high that you would have this heavenly trio for dessert. Nobody minded the repetition because, whether the meal was heavy or light, cocktail dress or shorts and tee shirts casual, Strawberries with Sour Cream and Brown Sugar was always the perfect ending. I'm not sure why it has gone out of style, but it is time to bring it back.

HERE'S A TIP: For fun, choose the large, stemmed strawberries guests can use to dip into the sugar and cream. Which is not to say that trimmed berries aren't just as good.

HERE'S ANOTHER TIP: If your brown sugar is hard and/or lumpy, put the box into the microwave for about 10 seconds to loosen it up. Exact time will depend on the power of your oven

COOKING PLAN: There is none, just put everything on a dessert plate and serve.

1 pint fresh strawberries, washed and hulled
1 cup sour cream
8 tablespoons lump-free brown sugar

Divide all ingredients equally on dessert plates and let your posse dig in.

Serves 4

Bon Appétit

Give How To Cook Healthy A Thumbs Up

Thank you so much for taking the time to read **How to Cook Healthy in a Hurry**. If you have enjoyed it, I would appreciate it if you would leave a positive review here: http://amzn.to/11mxCtk

Pick up your free gift

Please accept a free gift of 5 delicious and easy sugar free dessert recipes as my way of saying thank you for your interest in this book. Simply go to the link below and leave your email address so I can send these delectable desserts to you. In addition, from time to time, I will send you information on upcoming books and promotions that might interest you.

http://www.helencassidypage.com/how-to-cook-healthy-in-a-hurry-bonus/

Medical Disclaimer

The information in this book is for educational purposes only. It is not meant to provide or replace medical advice you may have received. If you are concerned about a medical or health issue, contact your health care provider immediately. If you are pregnant, have a major health issue, are under 18 or over 65, do not embark on any dietary changes without consulting your physician or other health care provider.

The dietary suggestions in this book are not meant to cure an illness. Your first line of defense in promoting good health is always a consultation with your health care provider. Feel free to discuss this book with your doctor or nutritionist and tailor the book and recipes to your own needs.

ABOUT ME

My publishing credits include writing two heart-healthy cookbooks with Stanford University cardiologist, John S. Schroeder, M.D. My work has appeared in Gourmet, Bon Appétit, Self Magazine and Men's Fitness, among other magazines. I have written many articles and online columns and have made numerous public cooking demonstrations as well as radio and TV appearances. For many years I ran my own cooking school and did menu consulting for restaurants.

Since this book first came out, I have released three additional books in the series. And if your sweet tooth is nagging at you, I am working on the world's greatest collection of desserts, just for a change of pace.

In addition, I have published three books for children.

My Author Page

Please read my author page for more information about me and my upcoming books and activities.

https://www.amazon.com/author/helencassidypage

Treat yourself to the other books in the How To Cook Healthy In A Hurry series

How To Cook Healthy In A Hurry, Volume 2

http://www.amazon.com/How-Cook-Healthy-Hurry-ebook/dp/B00C3OHEGE/

The Healthy Husband Cookbook

http://www.amazon.com/The-Healthy-Husband-Cookbook-ebook/dp/B00BEBOW8K/

The Soup Diet Cookbook

http://www.amazon.com/Soup-Diet-Cookbook-Delicious-ebook/dp/B00BRRZQC2/

Copyright Information